A Passion According to Green

Mark Irwin

New Issues Poetry & Prose

A Green Rose Book

New Issues Poetry & Prose
The College of Arts and Sciences
Western Michigan University
Kalamazoo, Michigan 49008

First Edition, 2017.

ISBN: 978-1-936970-49-0 (paperbound)

Library of Congress Cataloging-in-Publication Data:
Irwin, Mark.
A Passion According to Green/Mark Irwin
Library of Congress Control Number: 2016919574

Editor:	William Olsen
Managing Editor:	Kimberly Kolbe
Layout Editor:	Sarah Kidd
Assistant Editor:	Ephraim Sommers
Art Direction:	Nicholas Kuder
Design:	Deon Mixon
Production:	Paul Sizer
	The Design Center, Frostic School of Art
	College of Fine Arts
	Western Michigan University
Printing:	McNaughton & Gunn, Inc.

A Passion According to Green

Mark Irwin

New Issues

WESTERN MICHIGAN UNIVERSITY

Also by Mark Irwin

American Urn: Selected Poems (1987-2014)
Large White House Speaking
Tall If
Bright Hunger
White City
Quick, Now, Always
Against the Meanwhile: Three Elegies
The Halo of Desire

Essays:
Monster: Distortion, Abstraction, and Originality in Contemporary American Poetry

Translations:
Philippe Denis: *Notebook of Shadows*
Nichita Stanescu: *Ask The Circle To Forgive You: Selected Poems*

For Lisa Utrata & Mary Lou Irwin,

in memory of Cody Todd (1978-2016),

& for all those gone, the ghosts, still close, haunting the green.

Contents

IV.

"The excess over the present is the life of the Infinite."

—Emmanuel Levinas

"How many colors are there in a field of grass to the crawling baby unaware of 'green'?"

—Stan Brakhage

ONE

Events miniaturized, but always present

—Stumbling, tripping through dark, last night
we glimpsed the Crab Nebula. When a star

dies we call its shock of Technicolor
a supernova. Today a brute bumblebee

rumbles the wisteria's lilac clouds. Today
an infant and a zinnia. The one's crying becomes the other's

vivid color. Today cumuli, lightning, then
pollen floating on the pond like moments still spilling

from the Big Bang. —Gush of water, laughter, a hiccup. The zinnia seeds
resemble arrowheads. The tense

of all verbs is really the same. Why didn't I keep the letter sent
before you died unopened?

Lights

swimming the earth at dusk and prickling the distance
of the near town. In the jigsaw puzzle of the falls I could
feel a fine mist. Driving I think of it now—snapping those
last pieces in—and how history makes things small. The Apollo
Mission and moonwalk reduced to a few stock phrases. Finally
everything just seems made of words, but some call out to you.
Bees prowling the lobelia's sapphire falls, or that boy's arc of golden
piss. I once watched his unborn head crown and saw the prunish
face scream, reddening with seconds of air. The slick hair
smelled of roses still arriving, then his parents looked deeply
into each other's mouth for nights, days, years closing around
the swing set, bicycles and cars, the pots and pans in the kitchen,
the chipped china, glasses, and hanging spoons, and the way
the jam jars continue to gather that house's mansioning glow.

Primer

When I learned to write it was spring. For trees I drew
short vertical lines with a circle resting on each. For birds
I drew small X's in each circle. That autumn I learned
to read words—*trees, birds*—while letters blew like leaves
across the earth. Now I write pages of words but underneath
I still hear trees, birds, and sometimes I'll circle a word
or X out another, or other times the page will kite
beyond my hands like a swallow and I'll remember
to press harder into each furrow because time is brief
and words make us easy, and sometimes if someone dies
I'll climb a tree, make a circle round it with my arms,
forgetting about words, then scream long into the roots of things.

A Zipper

In an hour the stars still loading will swarm
like seconds found, and something

about stars was a song he lulled
us to sleep with, fifty years ago. *Ago*, the second half of that word
streaming into the *what*

was I fish back—silver and shaking now—or perhaps later at a red

light, as part of the streaming traffic
pauses, and for a moment those notes

flesh the present like migrant sand on a name chiseled

in stone. Sometimes
the margins of our lives seem unbearable, a zipper

against the dark we tear

open toward a gleam that briefly
devours. Recalling

that song I can almost fall asleep again, sleep in a steeper
sleep that moves like wind lifting a dried moth's wings.

Field Events

The sun with its invisible burin etches lines in our skin
while the trees rise, green spears, then collapse into scarlet.

I believed that language could save us from the temporal.

—Times of grief or joy when our faces opened entirely to one another.

What lies lost in the gutter between pages in every
book, the light and shadow cast from inside words.

*   *   *

—The calf and its mother slopping through creek and sopping grass.

The flesh of mountains is made of trees,
the flesh of words is carved from emotion.

—Now the accumulation of voices like a river. "You
were a stranger once..." "Yes, and so were you."

*   *   *

As one grows older it's of more and more importance to make the present larger,
but the past seems to grow much faster. It's as though you are painting a scene
while something rapidly occurs in the background to which everyone points.

*   *   *

The trout I caught, photographed, and ate, swims on my screensaver now.

*   *   *

At night the city generates heat and the beaches shine like radium.

As it grew colder, torn pieces of paper began falling from the sky. We
touched one another but had nothing to say. Eternity's
not a game on some board we play, but a slow selling off of the body.

Psalm

We are a small, quiet people, most of us less than 3" tall and can't speak unless
we chew on the grass—the grass that spreads for miles and years—then we speak
of mountains with massive pines, and of another people, tacit with faces made of
cloud, who with their one unspoken word hold us falling through their hands.

Open House

The realtor is whistling through the spacious rooms.

Everything's so new—floors, carpet, paint—as if just created.

There are cookies on the Plexiglas tray. —Coffee and tea.

There are flowers on the mantle. She wants us to feel at home.

A puzzle of a forest, unassembled, lies on an end table.

We pass a small box to each other. The last one

sets it down. Inside is a model of this house. We

all peer down a long way to see. Now a child lifts

the roof off. Inside are figures just like us. Our breaths

make clouds. This is the way our lives start. This is the way they go.

A Tiny Cage,

I'd found in the grass, and inside the cage

an even smaller mirror that I removed through the hinged

door, and in its polished square I saw a human

likeness leading others away from a city's tall monuments,

moments in our history. They too each carried a tiny cage

like this one, shimmering with light, as though filled with something

living. From what were they

fleeing as they sang of skyscrapers, bridges, condos,

malls, and billboards? And each one

carried an even smaller blue screen flickering with memory

or hope for that shining toward which hesitantly they kept walking.

If

If we knew as much as the trees, the hours and miles
of sap, sun. —But how? *Listen.* —Doorway to what? Memories
gone to chalk: You and *you* into the dark but the present's
still bustling, the fringe of each second sliding through grass, or
wind hustling a plastic bag down the street as April's chlorophyll
scent builds through the rain, and there in a distant sun-stabbed
tower, someone gazes down at cloth-gusseted folk streaming
in, out—just fine, just fine—while here ants gather granules,
doming the soil. If I were an Aztec, I might understand more
this *summarium* of light building above the silhouette
of peaks and clouds like cities. Sometimes the money floats
down and no one looks up, each body a little sack of flesh.
Sometimes I need to grip the earth, or sometimes I become tall
just to see what I'll never have but will give to others.

Two Horses

There were two horses, something I'll never forget.

I stood between them both and the soft doors of the earth.

It was early morning, their breaths steaming above frost.

It was late evening and their teeth cropped the tall grass.

It was winter, spring, summer, fall. I touched their manes and sweaty

flanks. There were two horses. They walked away then slowly turned.

One began to age rapidly while the other grew young. Two horses.

—A shoddy thing and a colt. I built a tall house between them,

where craving the earth I've lived ever since.

A vanilla cake,

with vanilla frosting, he'd made himself, he took

to his mother who lived alone on the mountain, where he walked

up the snowy steps under the masked pines. "Happy Birthday," he said,

as crouched she walked and set it on the empty table surrounded

by chairs and dozens of photographs. *Where are they?* she wondered,

making coffee, lighting a candle as her son made a fire, his hair the color of ice

she thought as they both sat down, the cake between them, into which

they buried their hands, touching. "It's still warm," she said. "Yes," he said,

as the wax dripped from the tall candle, and they talked. "How are things

in the valley?" she asked. "Still green," he said. "*Good, good,*" she said,

as they began to feed each other with their fingers, closing their eyes,

making wishes as the stars blazed through the big window, snow blowing

from the eaves as they ate, telling of the past, then moments of the present—

the weather and the heart—continuing to eat bigger handfuls, their faces white, smeared, till it

started to taste of something new and strange and far away.

Landscape Tapering Toward Infinity

The washing lifts in the wind beneath clouds. Each shirt or towel

gestures like a sentence beginning. Many times I have failed

with my body. August and the peaches fully pronounce

their yellows and reds, beginning to dissolve from outside

in. The washing lifts in the wind. The uneven song

of beginning. If you came this way in spring you would see

wind over clothes a freedom. I've been waiting a long time

in the sun. Inside the peach, flesh yellows to red

seed. Have you glimpsed the end? It's like the beginning

only with a full view. The sentence means more as it

continues. Now windows in nearby houses turn to water, flooding

the yards and streets, while laundry lofts, blows, and trees float by in the wind.

Luella

Today there's an exact weight to the light
like that of the sun crossing a lion's
body. Today we look
but can't find you. *A lifetime*, I say and remember nymphs of stoneflies
rising toward the river's surface. In dream you
are young and children run
across the hill of your shoulders. Sometimes you can see
a light coming from rocks. It burns
with an intensity once lost. The children, laughing, watch the lion
shake a piece of red meat in its mouth
then lie down to sleep: A disquiet, a light so bright
your eyes are wet with it.

On Earth

An astronaut could hear a baby crying
in the space ship. On earth it was autumn.
What season in space? He wanted to call
his wife, tell her about the crying. No one
else could hear it, though it often seemed
closer, but always receding, like ice breaking
up in spring. He thought he remembered
when he was an infant and last night dreamed
of a milk made from water and powdered
bone. He drank a lot of it and the crying grew
louder. Within he could hear a faint humming
like the tines of a rake. In autumn humans
like to make big piles of leaves, on earth as it is.

Peeling

the potato I remember how long it took you

to come back from the dead, from the stupor of mud and exhaustion

of ash. The apples you dispatched in dream were right on cue

with the hawk whistling over pines and over my bed

till your volutes of speech turned in the air and a bank of stars

throbbed above. The smell of sulfur

lingered from a mine into which a child was shoveling

snow. I think of everything now, the space between a shattered

glass and a glacier's fracture through which your

hand reached, an animal all itself made of time, then I read

your note, the poverty of words—sounds eager—

then and now, fleeing over the page.

A book—

I keep on my bed, a red
book with not many pages, though the pages
are wide like the sheets at night

when I sleep, if I sleep and am not thinking about the book, what
I left out, the weight of those things
missing, the words in the red book, the ones I said

in my mind now part
of the book that in sunlight seems almost human on the white sheets, the red
book blushing, or that at dusk

looks like a scab under which I sometimes hear a murmuring, or the mewling
of an animal, so I'll sleep on top of the book
or put it next to my

ear, or move it over my body. If it
was your book what
would you do?

TWO

A fly

zings through the century of a window all day
till dusk, then finds a light bulb to orbit. Yesterday
in the hospital I marveled at the newborns, pink
sacks of time, their faces scrunched with the future's
weight. Walking outside now, beyond the baled
alfalfa, I gaze up where a comet dashes like a mouse
across the kitchen floor of heaven, and there, just below
the Belt of Orion, the photo-ionized gas of the Trapezium
Cluster glows part red blood cell, part luminous wing.
As we get older each look in the mirror gets farther. "Come
back," they say. On the third floor of the ward I sat with Lonnie,
head shaved like a monk's, talking about that pond
in Pennsylvania where we once as lovers swam. Now
I stare and would like to part the glass of this sky's window.

Firenze Pietà

On her knees, face thrust toward concrete, she

couldn't get low enough, hands outstretched, rattling

coins in a Styrofoam cup while the black cat with white back

legs moonwalked in the shadow of stairs as Vespas

darted near her, curbed in the beknighted

day. Later a tattooed pig

wattled between rows of gold necklaces on the Ponte

Vecchio. Flavio said

she was eighty, had taught

in the church before losing her daughter. Thunder, then rain slaughtering

the Arno. When I returned she was still

there, sopping wet like a tissue and her cup was

brimming with water from

which she drank.

Zoo

In her old age, mother enjoys going to the zoo
as the trees let loose their yellow leaves
and stand like furniture among the grazing animals
who stare from a long distance. Often I think
this could be a story she's telling me as we walk
through doorways catching fire, or sit on a stone bench
growing larger and more cold, watching the little clouds
our words make, and in the distance—buffalo, built
of the earth, with their horns made of rock, their coats
of dried grass. "Only drama without movement
is beautiful," said Simone Weil, speaking of Lear, and soon
everything's ablaze and we're running toward youth,
and the skyline of a city, its fossil, while animals, shrieking,
stampede past us, and mother calls out their names,
zebra, *buffalo*, *gazelle*, ever so clearly, then enters
into shadow with them, that diorama we call memory.

The words,

their small emotions

grating on sound, their vowels siphoning

history. —Or tomorrow reaching

its dusk sleeve. "Hello, Wait, Please,"

I once said, trying to open flesh with ghost-sounds

threading themselves through

infinity, the knot of past

voices choiring while I try to gobble

its babble in memory. One July we drank a glass

of water then set it down

in the god-heat of grass. Ants, gnats, and a stunned moth

remind the dumb math

of years, the tacit

hours and how the pronoun *I* keeps

fraying, digging like a mole through smells: sweat

on a watch band, a scarf, or sock

scouting a drawer. Some old cards the cat

pulls down. On a shirt the wrong

button you sewed now casually

chatting with some ashes I keep postponing to loose

in the wind of your fled

laughter, clear, jetting forth, syllabic, unrehearsed and taller

than any grief.

I wanted to tell about the weight of it,

something you might feel in a blueprint, curled and yellowed,
or in the heft of voices rising in a crowd.

Before she died we bought a green ladder. She put her shoes
under it at night as if practicing for something else.

If you open a wound and look carefully among the oranges & reds
there is a circle in which hundreds of balls fit. They

could be from a miniature carnival where people are laughing,
or at a birthday party in the future.

Now I hang clothes over the ladder and the dusk sky's
the color of gently hammered brass.

Somewhere people are taking an elevator up and down in a tall
building and the blueprint still lies in the drawer.

It was the weight of it we didn't know we had borne,
that the ladder was a telescope of sorts, and if you looked into the distance

you could see people walking through one another, an old man
through a boy become an infant carried in a mother's receding arms.

Powder

Yesterday I opened your pill box and, there

on one oblong chalk tablet, read with my finger

the laws by which we live—*love, love—and* with a pin's

chisel wanted to carve more while your wrist

skirted that dark and the cupidon of our past gazed down.

A Passion According to Green

In my sleep a small boy approached,
all green, holding out his hands. He'd
come far from the mountains, a little
snow on his collar. He asked if
I could see, and though I wasn't sure
what he meant, I said, yes, then he
asked me to follow. How can I tell
you how many springs, April
after April till we came to a great
fire, blue at its base into which he
walked, smiling, turning in sunlight
through rain, a thousand years in
a moment, a little snow on the mountain.

Speed of Light

Married in Beijing, they had their names carved on

a grain of rice. Mai wore a yellow silk gown. He wore

a black suit. Embraced in the photo turned sideways

they resemble a tiger scrambling through strewn mums.

That evening they ate salted mango and shrimp. He

can still taste that, see the tortoise shell clip sun-

splintered in her hair. That evening continues, stalled

like the sea-filled drapes in their room. For twenty

years he worked at a lab that accelerated protons. Here

are photographs of their two girls on Lake Michigan,

then in Zermatt, standing before the Matterhorn,

whose moraines, cirques, and ravines resemble those

through two names magnified on a grain of rice, or

of that shadow looming through the CAT scan of her brain.

View

To be on fire look at the green skull of a mantis

in spring. Burst of pollen from a pine

bough. Dug a hole for the dog. Dug and dug

in the earth till my red coat shone, far

in the earth where a mountain grew. Farther

than I've ever climbed, then looked at the gibbous

moon. Events grow small. Stamp

of a giraffe now extinct in Sumatra: 500,000

humans dead. One survivor beat the horn of an ox into

a brown window just to see into the ground.

The Length of Water

For Alain Borer

Like you they waited a long time

for the boat arriving at dusk. Like you

they were tired and stepped from the dock

onto its bow then took their seats, looking out

at water that coursed like words

as the boat grew longer

over the night and they waited

all their lives while their bodies

grew, so they didn't notice they weren't

moving, as the boat moved like a sentence with no

meaning and they became a likeness

of themselves, a reflection across the water

that once swirled inside them too

now motionless as that boat connecting two shores.

Gladiolus

After your death I was looking at

gladiolus, white gladiolus, their fast petals

climbing the air. Their task a ladder, bridge,

while outside cattle grazed, crazy their hunger for grass

as clouds scuttled toward the horizon, bunching up

like *glads*. Cattle drank from a pond while those petals

vaulted from the vase, stalked Yeses, and looking at them now

I'm drinking from a shattered glass, the one etched with

your name, the one that sails on and on, pushed up

by its vowels as these petals push up the past then

let it drop. *What, what, what,* they say, a likeness

of vowels blowing, naming a ghost. The task is

often one of beauty: long stems of an epiphanic

white. When the blossoms died, cattle fed on the stalks.

Poof!

A shark swims into the bay, swirls, and then rises with the ugly grin of millennia.

A match flame to a cigar, years later a campfire, and long after a house on fire.

Love—to forget language and act on instinct, its indestructible form.

—Something written on a piece of paper after an astonishing event. That paper found a long time later.

I am, *I am*, she said, licking a grape Popsicle in July. *Make it last*, he said right after.

It seemed as though she had leapt toward her own cremation.

A few books shining like the wood of trees. —Ones that I've climbed or held.

Threshold

It was the way the cat, which for 20 years always greeted them at the door, continued to greet them after it went blind and had to walk along the wall now, and they would wait by the door till the cat, sometimes taking ten minutes, arrived.

I thought about it yesterday, coming home after many years, the furniture covered with sheets, the photographs pressed neatly against the walls. I stood a long time, letting the past trickle back to shadow, till my feet turned black and I walked away leaving footprints.

The cat carved the body of space by clinging to the walls, the only way it could make the space larger, preparing its owners as they waited, longer by the door.

Did I say that I took a white sheet off the chair and sat down? Did I say it snowed, melted, then snowed again in that room while the furniture grew and the cat began pushing its head into the corners as if it could go through the walls, the pictures of four generations?

It moved more and more slowly. We stood by the door waiting longer. We are waiting there still, neither late nor early, only now.

Where

my July cap had blown
by the cliff's edge an
old mine shaft's scaffold
half collapsed and below
one timber a small tin
can with cut lid closed on
some paper all wound
in plastic I unfurl
to find a photo of
Elsie, 1910, "to John

with love, Ever," the ink
coursing, coursing like
Chalk Creek now— "and when
we marry," it says. I put it
back—can, lid, plastic—ten
years ago, a kind of
bell you can hear when
ever light strikes the mountain.

Twist-O-Flex

A cheap band that rode his wrist for twenty years. One

you could twist, bend, but not break, an eclectic

design whose gold plating wore off with his life. Grief

and joy settled in the watch face: two bright hands swept

the hours to years in its sealed crystal where what

we call time, all those whims in a caught

wind whirled. I would wear it, but changing the band

could smell him there on each accordion *twiston*

blade catching mirco- scopic bits of hair, skin. I've

kept it in a plastic sandwich bag inside another all

these years. Sometimes I try, opening one

bag, the other, then place my face there to breathe.

Listen, listen,

a voice shied with light, and the budded
aspens gilded with late

snow melting: the greening heart of it. Watching,
you might ask, *How many*

dead have I touched? The moths dazed on the porch this morning,
their burnt vellum, their fury
of seconds, hours while the body

of stars sawed about like a great animal in that incandescent
pasture. Who will lead you
by the hackamore through sleep—matter unanswered—

to that barn without walls?

THREE

Otherwise Than Our Bodies

—White caps of peaks incandescent in sunlight and strophes of cloud.
Wind long there and our breath
here. Years, St. Mary's

Glacier receding. We walked its blinding glare—ice and snow
at noon etching a slow
text on stone—

then headachy and sunburned went home.

      * * *

—House, each with its petals of doors and windows.
Each one growing smaller and smaller till gone.

      * * *

Lake O'Haver at dusk, the silken parachute of fish guts by our feet, I watched
the sky turn red where peaks rose in the jellied light
as trout flashed from our lines.

Or above White Creek the black bears that rolled big rocks down on the jeep trail.
We laughed, drinking beer, watching it on the night camera.

      * * *

Outside Lake George, the Hayman fire had been burning for months, and one day
three gold bodies—boys—dove from a rock into a pool of flame, then climbed out,
shivering in their violet skin. "Are

you from Green?" they asked. "Yes," I said, as the evening sun leaned, mirroring
itself through smoke while slowly they danced, glimmering
like something astral in the autumn

of their youth. Then I could not see, and like a child asked through the darkness,
"Where are you?" and they said, "Just on the other side of where you stand."

                    *   *   *

At the ranch, in the tall grass by the well house, one June I find a sickle, its dull blade
speckled with rust. The handle, carved from pine, holds two brass rivets, eyes
looking far into the field. I take

it to the barn and with whetstone begin sharpening, honing the blade
till its curve's a clean-lit horizon. Later, walking
alongside the ditch by the well,

I put it back for someone else to find, the blade shining like water, the entire day gone.

* * *

In Ohio once, body to body, after moving through each other
for hours, we fumbled outside to watch kids at play
while the November sun pushed low

at noon. Screaming, running, laughing, they strove and strove—
giants in their small fenced world.

It's desire we keep shoveling in memory, down to the last teaspoonful.

    * * *

The white steeple slaving blue air or sometimes a mountain, the white steeple
where a crow lands, aperture through which this snapshot congeals again.

    * * *

One October evening, walking through a dry riverbed, we can still feel
April's bearded pull. Great cottonwoods and willows fill the day's pink shell,

and I remember the man who planted kernels of corn—
a thousand years old—he'd found in an archeological cave.

Three months later the small green ears sprang like verbs from the dark.

Tonight from the black stem of sky the stars burst open like pods, all salt and shivering
form, when through the visible, glimpses of the invisible are gained.

    * * *

—Dawn. —Full-blown sun daubing the cows, their god-weight on the land.

And now the bleating of sheep, frogs, as the earth falls back
through our bodies and we walk far into the speaking world.

*   *   *

Feeling her first teeth through pink gums and finding no words.
—Rags of sunlight, left by a rooster's cry, rearranging the dusty air.

—Trout, pink and violet-sided, slit jaw to ass, still quaking on the grass.
—The moss smell through aspen and alder.

*   *   *

If I could remember more the snow would carve a thousand sopping meadows.

*   *   *

—Or Richard and I at the quarry in rain, Richard touching the granite
he would cut and polish, Richard who now has
no body.

*   *   *

Poetry has something to do with our bodies, flesh the soft wall we want to enter,
so as to create and give it names.

Otherwise we would not push dark letters, allowing the words to cut and suture.

I want to touch the moment with all its scars, to lift both consonant and vowel
as the irises open in daylight, and the pollen lingers on the slow kite of the page.

* * *

A feather sticks to the branch of a cedar through rain, winds and hail,
through spring and summer.

A neighbor gives birth to a child, and a war begins and ends in Iraq.

Above, clouds pass. The sun sets and rises many times and names slip like tags
off lives I know. Still, the feather holds, its tether

a soft nail. Birds fly south. On a nearby limb a chrysalis becomes a moth.
Leaves flash, startling us with yellow, as though a window of green had shattered.

* * *

Just before the end of Mahler's 9th, one hears the violins shear upward in a sudden wing
of grief as the body gasps, then a stillness within a stillness
builds an immeasurable height.

* * *

Time, how we toss in the sleep of its wind.

* * *

Far into April, far into its green knives and teeth, the sun illumines
the gauze of leaves lifting something

in us all, while light builds, layering the evening pond
that with the gold mouth of a trumpet
says and continues

to say *Yes*.

FOUR

There's a jet

in my mouth that devours words.

We were having a barbecue when the neighbor

said Jeff had been electrocuted while washing the car.

Upstairs I could see the corpse laid out on their new

drive. "I'm sorry," I say later and the jet puffs toward

Ray, Jeff's Dad. He opens his mouth and turns away

to the little forest by the freeway. Now the turbine

in his throat whirs till the jet rises, circling our neighborhood.

We all look up and point while a deer walks near

our houses, past the flat screens in picture windows, past

our motorcycles and cars. The deer's hungry and can sense

the new wilderness in that yard. The pastor arrives. Everyone

looks down as the jet circles higher over roofs and power

lines. The car shines next to the dead body. Now

they must clean and dress it up, then put it in the ground. Look,

someone says, a deer, and I place it next to the jet, humming on the page.

Whatever

they are doing there together, they are digging

a large hole and filling it with light. Sometimes just a match

or lamp-shine while others lift armfuls of streaming sun. Men

are talking there, whispering as though they'd found pieces

of the heart, shards glittering toward tomorrow where they would

be free, but here they learn something about time that only

a hand can tell you. How it opens or closes, giving and taking.

They will miss the dark but only as they will sleep's colossal

view of memory, and how love is always the final story,

whether anthill or mountain, one travels the same distance

across some heaven or the vellum of a page, where finally one

must choose between word and the steep white it rests upon,

where we live now, telling stories of the dark in its glare

as the letters fade and we look through one another then see.

Weight

I was chasing a red ball across the lawn when the trees
began growing and I saw you

in a mirror, the silver light tossed back and forth
by friends, family, a wedding

where we sang, ate, growing older as the day expired. How is it
we know totality

only in dark? You moved through summer and while you were dying
I was stung by a bee, a moment of pain so full

its brief gold lit the day. To place joy and worry
in a box. To leave

then return and call it a house. To sleep and upon waking
find childhood there, all its toys

crippled until the sparks of music waken them, voiced in an instant so long
we can feel the trees pressed into stone.

Safety Pin

I must have carried it around for 15 years

in my shaving kit, hoping to use it sometime

but never did until one day on a plane this guy

next to me asked if I happened to have a safety pin?

Sure, I said, and stood up to take it out of my luggage.

He'd torn his shirt—no big deal—but it was on the shoulder

where he couldn't reach. I held the pin up like a tiny sword

then went to work, bending toward him as if to whisper

something. "I'm dying," he said, stone-faced.

What, I said. "That's why I'm going to Cleveland, a final

experiment for my shot kidneys." Dialysis? I asked. "For years,"

he said, holding a long cord, looped at both ends

on his lap. He fingered it like a rosary. What's that? I asked.

"It's a bow string," he said. "I'm an archer." Wow, I said, leaning

back toward him, tucking, re-pinning the tear, then patting

his shoulder. "I started with a toy bow my father gave me,

rubber-tipped arrows and all. Now I've been to tournaments

all over the world," he added, then his head dropped, even though the plane

seemed to be climbing as the sun broke through clouds, catching

his body. Slowly I slipped my finger through one loop of

the cord and I pulled and he pulled till it was taut.

Three Stories

When the cat was dying, sitting on his haunches

in the dusk sun, he told me the story of a mouse.

Come closer, the cat said, and I did till my breath

moved the fur on his neck. It was an old mouse,

he said, one hardly worth catching but I did.

The cat was breathing heavier now. I reached for him

but he said, No, and continued. *Let me go,*

the mouse yelped, *please, for I am old and just awoke*

when you caught me. So what, I said, pinning him

on the ground with the pads of my two paws. *Let me*

tell you a story, the mouse said, so I listened. *I have*

come to my age through many doors, more than

you, and it is I who tell dreams to other mice. You

must let me go! Tell me a dream, I told the mouse,

and it was then the mouse began growing, growing

until finally I felt only the tail where that enormous

shadow pooled. *The days are as long or as short as you want,*

the mouse said, and I let him go, though I didn't understand,

as now you don't understand, so faraway so close.

One of your wisdom teeth,

kept in a jar on my desk since a decade ago

you decided to embark from this world. How

many times did my tongue brush against it?

Once I put it in my mouth and felt its dim

flare summon the years, and sometimes

the tooth is an iceberg and I'm in a small boat

touching its walls, or sometimes it's a waterfall near

which I'm soaked, looking up as its curtains open

to subtitles I'm trying to read, and sometimes

the tooth is a cloud among other clouds brushing

the trees, but in my hand I hold the real tooth,

the one that smells like a stone set in fire, a stone covered in snow

from which a red light pulses like an ancient rose.

Sometimes,

I'll crumple the paper before beginning to write
on it, or sometimes I'll spray my notebook with water,
then sit in the sun, jabbing at the muggy pages with
a pencil. Each does what he can to make this process
more difficult, and why not? The white paper's selfish,
wanting only more space and silence, inviting words
as one might houses to an Alaskan glacier, or inviting
emotions as one might guests to a wedding, each of them
blindfolded, feeling their way into the chapel to listen,
then toward the buffet to eat. And sometimes I'll write on black
paper—the letters glinting, barely detectable, deterring my desire
to change things—then tilt the paper at noon to read it.
And sometimes I'll toss the empty pages into the fire
at dusk and speak to them as one would to a child, or
a ghost ruining the sky, then only what I wake to
in the old morning will I remember.

Spring

I'd been traveling a long time away from cities into the mountains. Pausing, he said,
"Finally you must give everything away," then he pushed a green square into my hand.
It was the model of a house, something you would find on a cheap game board. I walked
until evening then dug a small hole and buried it. In the morning, other houses had risen
next to my tent, and tiny people whistled, going to and fro through the grass. I felt very old
but happy, thinking of those gone and how the dead pull the new dead toward them while
we remember, allowing them to grow. Meanwhile those houses continued to spring up
and the grass grew taller until I seemed one with those people, and with the grass from
which they built their houses, so many houses round which they hummed.

For Your Viewing Pleasure

Think of the TV as a kind of jar placed in our

living rooms. We were wearing our red coats. We were wearing

our blue, yellow, and green ones. We were

Technicolor. We put hours,

days into the jar while our children place baubles, dolls,

candy, coins there. —An argosy of sorts. He believes

his wife conceived in front of the TV. I laughed but felt

incredibly lonely as when touching

a fossil. Have you ever been in a room

with it when no one's around? Have you ever looked at the planet

Mars through a telescope? Once I stood

in an empty cattle car, after they'd been unloaded

for slaughter, and walked back and forth, trying to look out

the slats. My daughter reaches

into the jar and begins eating the toy figures

like chocolate, then laughing, appears older, naked and busty

on the big screen. "A loneliness like that?" he asked. "Yes,"

I said, "like that!"

The Rat

was the color of tar and in his tail I could feel

all the wires of the city. He had woken me from sleep and sat next

to the porcelain sink, eating a loaf of whole grain bread.

He stuck his rat muzzle through the plastic bag, then pressed

the loaf against the wall, eating, pushing, eating until he'd consumed

it all, and the empty bag just floated there, filled with his rat breath, then he

started shitting little turds in the white sink, as if he were writing me

a rat poem. My girlfriend woke and screamed. We were to be married

that June. The rat was like a hole in something good. When he ate, his teeth

made a humming sound like that of electric current gone bad. He must have come

in through the window opening onto the roof. St. Augustine says the origin

of evil is free will. *If only I could reach that cantaloupe*, I thought, then

the sudden feeling that I was in a cage and needed to draw an opening

on the wall. Paunchy, he stood on his hind legs and looked at me. My girlfriend

screamed again, this time from the car in the drive. Her father was my dentist. No more

need be said. *Wait*, I shrieked to her one last time as the rat crawled out

the kitchen window onto the roof, where in the moonlight

he looked up, cackling at stars.

the stars with their come-ons,

each one axled, invisibly
upward. All night over I-70, Orion floats east to west: Moab,

Capitol Reef, Zion. *An old starling, one among many*
squawking in snowed pines, fell down, trying

its wings among creaking boughs. Cataract of dusk-gold
in its eyes, dull hackles and worn

tail feathers. The woman had brushed close in Vegas and tried

to steal my wallet. Inside the last
picture of you. *I opened*

then closed the wings in snow, the bellows of its balked black
belly up, blowing, sieving

what distant, spangled want.

Household

The man kept a grey box in the basement. He kept

it in the bottom drawer of a green filing cabinet and occasionally

he would ask the boy to come down into

the basement where he would open the box as each sat

on opposite sides of the desk. The man would lay

the contents of the box—mortgage, life insurance, bank books—

between them and say, "One day you'll need to open these

documents. All the instructions are on this card." The boy

didn't like looking at the card and always looked down. One day

when the boy was getting ready to leave for the army

the man called the boy into the basement and as

he set the box between them, the boy took a smaller

box from his pocket and placed it next to the larger one.

The man smiled but the boy did not and opened

his box. Inside were several small rifles, all

pencil-sized and the boy and the man took turns

shooting each other with these, laughing,

leaving pinpricks of blood on each other till the woman

upstairs ran down, snapping her bath towel, naked, saying,

"Is this what both of you have made from me?"

Famous

A wedding by the river: stripling groom and a girl-

bride. A priest dressed in leaves read from texts of

clouds, then we toasted when the brown bear, lumbering, slopped

across the river and turning, growled in which I could hear

the word *Ursus*, the groom saying *yes, yes,* laughing, running

thru saplings, years, second growth forests with her toward

peaks near the Alma Mine, famous for a rhodochrosite

cleaved-rhomboid- shape, cherry- jello-colored specimen. *Thief*

of affection, thief *of extinction,* the mating call saves

us. The gem, from manganese-dissolved, combining with carbonate

then drips off caves underground: Gorgeous end of a tortuous event.

Ritual

I like saying the alphabet in a graveyard,

feeling each letter rise from stone, watching

the eyes of birds touching air and the acorns

drop from the sky. Now I can almost see stars

on the backs of the beetles' black shells, each

with its suitcase of trees, each having seen

into stone as the red skirt of dusk crouches

upon so many hidden sparks older than language.

Table of Contents

When the light, pummeled gold, casts the windows of houses up like foil

and the dusk begins to soften your bones toward snow

as you sit, turning photos in the album, each one

a hinge, or wing, the soft black feathers

sleeping under there, and the page another hinge,

and the book another in the creaking house

on the earth with its creaking trees, then you, too,

can step out into the darkness

onto the vast gleaming page of passing through.

Travel

At the border between living

and dying a red

mouth, pursed, whistles

no alarums, nor does it wish

to kiss, only to stretch the air from every spoken word

so that each one collapses there

into the darkness, a deep well, a mute

inverted Babel, but if unknowingly, you were

to place your ear against those

lips, what you would hear

would be a great party of vowels racing through names

and the names of things, a great wind

which pushes the sail of each face

through what we call

a life.

Acknowledgments

Many thanks to the editors of the following journals where these poems first appeared:

Academy of American Poets: "Poof!"

Agni Review: "A Tiny Cage," "Table of Contents"

Alaska Quarterly: "Where"

American Poetry Review: "The Rat"

Boston Review: "The words,"

Blackbird: "Peeling," "Twist-O-Flex"

Columbia: "Ritual," "Spring," "Two Horses"

Conjunctions: "If"

Denver Quarterly: "View"

Field: "Open House," "There's a jet"

Fifth Wednesday: "On Earth"

Great River Review: "I wanted to tell about the weight of it,"

Hotel Amerika: "A Passion According to Green," "Threshold," "The Length of Water"

Lana Turner: "Famous"

The Literary Review: "Household," "Three Stories"

Missouri Review (online feature): "Otherwise Than Our Bodies"

New American Writing: "*Listen, listen,*" "Psalm," "Travel"

New Letters: "Firenze Pietà"

New Ohio Review: "Speed of Light"

Pleiades: "Field Events," "For Your Viewing Pleasure," "One of your wisdom teeth," "Whatever"

Plume: "A book—," "Powder," "A Zipper," "Safety Pin"

Poetry Daily: "Zoo," "Lights" (Feb. 16, 2016)

Poetry Flash: "Landscape Tapering Toward Infinity"

Poetry International: "A vanilla cake," "Luella"

The Southern Review: "Lights," "Zoo"

Tin House: "A fly" "Primer"

Volt: "the stars with their come-ons,"

Photo by Steve Cohn

Mark Irwin is the author of nine collections of poetry, which include *A Passion According to Green* (2017), *American Urn: Selected Poems* (2015), *Large White House Speaking* (2013), *Tall If* (2008), *Bright Hunger* (2004), *White City* (2000), *Quick, Now, Always* (1996), and *Against the Meanwhile: Three Elegies* (1988). He has also translated Philippe Denis' *Notebook of Shadows* and Nichita Stanescu's *Ask the Circle to Forgive You: Selected Poems*. His poetry and essays have appeared in many literary magazines including *The American Poetry Review, Agni Review, The Atlantic Monthly, Georgia Review, The Kenyon Review, Paris Review, Pleiades, Poetry, The Nation, New England Review, New American Writing, The New Republic,* and *The Southern Review*. His collection of essays, *Monster: Distortion, Abstraction, and Originality in Contemporary American Poetry*, will appear in 2017. Recognition for his work includes The Nation/ Discovery Award, four Pushcart Prizes, two Colorado Book Awards, the James Wright Poetry Award, and fellowships from the National Endowment for the Arts, and the Fulbright, Lilly, and Wurlitzer Foundations. He is an associate professor in the PhD in Creative Writing & Literature Program at the University of Southern California and lives in Los Angeles and Colorado.